LIFE FULL OF UPS AND DOWNS

LIFE FULL OF UPS AND DOWNS

The Theme: Live and let live
The Writer:

Brother Cedric D. Anderson

ISBN:	Softcover	978-1-6641-5867-2
	eBook	978-1-6641-5866-5

Print information available on the last page.

Rev. date: 02/16/2021

To order additional copies of this book, contact:
Xlibris
844-714-8691
www.Xlibris.com
Orders@Xlibris.com
825233

Life full of ups and downs

Hi my name is Cedric D. Anderson about to tell you the story concerning life full of ups and downs. I been reminded of the late great gospel song writer by the name of Mahalia Jackson she wrote the song (Trouble will soon be gone trouble of the world.) Their's another gospel song writer someone I once look up to and he was a great influence to me his name the late James Cleveland he wrote the song (Trouble don't last always.)

When Morning Comes

Song Writer: Unknown

Trials dark on every hand and we cannot understand all the ways that God will lead us to that blessed promised land; but he'll guide us with his eye, and we'll follow till we die, we will understand it better by and by.

Life full of ups and downs

Some things will change, some things will not change. Some things we can except, some things we cannot except, some things hard to except; some things we don't want to except in some degree we're set in our ways.

Some people not gonna change they're set in their ways.

The point is you can lead the horse to the water but you can't make him drink it; let him use his own judgement.

Life full of ups and downs

I know their's a whole lots things in this society we have no control over we got to let go and let God have his way so we got to live and let live, and pray to the Father (Help me to move on in life and help me to except some thing that I cannot change.)

Psalms 121:1 I will lift up my eyes unto the hill from whence cometh my help.
Verse:2-My help come from the Lord who made heaven and earth.

John 14:1-Let not your heart be troubled: you believe in God, believe also in me

Verse:27-Peace I leave with you, my peace I give to you: not as the world giveth, give I unto you, let not your heart be troubled, neither let it be afraid.

John 16:33-The things I have spoken unto you, that in me ye might have peace. In the world ye shall have tribulation: but be of good cheer; I have overcome the world.

Romans 8:31-What shall we then say to these things? If God be for us, who can be against us?

Verse:35-Who shall separate us from the love of Christ? Shall tribulation, or distress, or persecution, or famine, or nakedness or peril, or sword?

Verse:36-As it is written, for thy sake we are killed all day long: we are accounted as sheep for the slaughter.

Life full of ups and downs

The life full of ups and downs fight the good fight of faith.

I Timothy 6:12-Fight the good fight of faith, lay hold on eternal life, where unto thou art also called, and hast professed a good profession before many witnesses

II Timothy 4:7-I have fought a good fight; I have finished my course, I have kept the faith.

I Peter 5:8-Be sober, be vigilant: because your adversary the devil, as a roaring lion, walketh about, seeking whom he may devour:

I Peter 4:16-Yet if any man suffer as a christian, let him not be ashamed; but let him glorify God on this behalf.

James 4:7-Submit yourselves therefore to God. Resist the devil, and he will flee from you.

Life full of ups and downs (Friendship of the world)

James 4:4-Ye adulterers and adulteresses know ye not that the friendship of the world is enmity with God? Whosoever therefore will be a friend of the world is the enemy of God.

Life full of ups and downs (Friendship of the World)

What are friendship of the world?

Galatians 5:19-21

Works of the flesh are manifest, which are these:

1. Adultery
2. Fornication
3. Uncleanness
4. Lasciviousness
5. Idolatry
6. Witchcraft
7. Hatred
8. Variance
9. Emulation
10. Wrath
11. Strife
12. Seditions
13. Heresies
14. Envying
15. Murders
16. Drunkenness
17. Revelling

Tug of war between Flesh and Spirit Galatians 5:17

Galatians 5:17-For the flesh lusteth against the Spirit, and the Spirit against the flesh: and these are contrary the one to the other: so that ye cannot do the things that ye would.

The cares of the world

I John 2:15-Love not the world, neither the things that are in the world. If any man love the world, the love of the Father is not in him

Verse:16-For all that is in the world, the lust of the flesh, and the lust of the eyes, and the pride of life, is not of the Father, but is of the world.

Verse:17-And the world passeth away, and the lust thereof: but he that doeth the will of God abideth for ever.

Matthew 13:22-He also that received seed among the thorns is he that heareth the word: and the care of this world, and the deceitfulness of riches, choke the word, and he becometh unfruitful.

Between Carnal and Spiritually minded

Romans 8:6-8

Romans 8:6-For to be carnally minded is death: but to be spiritually minded is life and peace.

Verse:7-Because the carnal mind is enmity against God: for it is not subject to the law of God, neither indeed can be.

Verse:8-So then they that are in the flesh cannot please God.

I Corinthians 2:13-Which things also we speak, not in the words which man's wisdom teacheth, but which the Holy Ghost teacheth; comparing spiritual things with spiritual.

Life full of ups and downs

Family Relationship

You ever heard this saying? I was 12 years old my mother said this it stuck with me as growing up it still with me this very day I will tell you what she said when she said that she said it with a authority (Family that pray together stay together) that's powerful talk never be forgotten. Have you ever heard the saying about family pulling together (Blood is thicker than water) that's a true saying; we may fight like cats and dogs don't know which one of us the cat; and which one of us dog; we might not agree on everything that don't mean we not family we will always be family no matter what happen there is no better time we need each other we need each other now you can't live in this world by yourself it once was a time I thought I can I was more set in my ways learned the hard that I can't; I remember one day I was talking to my uncle he and my aunt set me down and talk to me they ask me think you can live in this world by yourself? They pointed out a scripture to me that was Genesis 2:18 (And the Lord God said it is not good that the man should alone; I will make him an help meet for him.) That was a time they gave me a good talking to.

Life full of ups and downs

Your Spiritual Family

Spiritual family we should be about our brother and sister keepers. Quoting from the NKJV

John 13:34-A new commandment I give to you, that you love one another: as I have love you, that you also love one another.

Verse:35-By this all will know that you are my disciples, if you have love for one another.

I Corinthians 12:25-That there should be no schism in the body but that the members should have the same care for one another.

Verse:26-And if one member suffers, all the members suffer with it: or if one member is honored, all the members rejoice with it.

Verse:27-Now you are the body of Christ, and members individually.

Galatians 6:2-Bear one another's burdens, and so fulfill the law of Christ.

I Corinthians 14:40-Let all things be done decently and in order.
That's God call the shots

Life full of ups and downs

Let the beauty of Jesus be seen in you

According to familiar Hymn (Let the beauty of Jesus be seen in me.)

Matthew 5:16-Let your light so shine before men, that they may see your good works and glorify your Father in heaven.

Remind me of a song writer the late great Mahalia Jackson she wrote (smile when you happy smile when you sad good that you do coming back to you don't cost very much.)
The name of the song [Don't cost very much]

Life full of ups and downs some thing we got to live with I know it's not fare, I know this something you dis-agree with, that's society we can't control that but to let go let God have his way; 1970 Copyright David Ruffin and the Temptations written the song (Ball of confusion that what the world is today)

I Corinthians 14:33-For God is not the author of confusion but of peace, as in all the churches of the saints.

Hebrews 12:14-Follow peace with all men, and holiness, without which no man shall see the Lord:

In society we got to live and let live some things will change some things will not change as I said earlier, we're seeking our own righteousness.

Romans 10:3-For they being ignorant of God's righteousness, and going about to establish their own righteousness, have not submitted themselves unto the righteousness of God.

Life full of ups and downs

Love your enemies

Matthew 5:10-Blessed are they which are persecuted for righteousness' sake: for theirs is the kingdom of heaven.
Verse:11-Blessed are ye, when men shall revile you, and persecute you, and shall say all manner of evil against you falsely, for my sake.
Verse:12-Rejoice, and be exceeding glad: for great is your reward in heaven: for so persecuted they the prophet which were before you.
Verse:44-But I say unto you, love your enemies, bless them that curse you, do good to them that hate you, and pray for them which despitefully use, and persecute you;

Matthew 6:14-For if ye forgive men their trespasses, your heavenly Father will also forgive you:
Verse:15-But if ye forgive not men their trespasses, neither will your Father forgive your trespasses.

When Jesus hung there on the cross what did he said to his Father in heaven?
Luke 24:34-Then said Jesus, Father; forgive them; for they know not what they do. And they parted his raiment and cast lots.

It don't pay to hate individual but, you don't hath to like their ways.

<u>Life full of ups and downs</u>

<u>Being considered of others</u>

Being considered of others take each other seriously, respect each other's feelings, treat others the way you wish to be treated.

What honestly offends me which that's dangerous which an average individual don't take to heart is <u>teasing another individual</u> some people ask me (why you don't show humor?) I'll give you 4 reason why

1. It offend me (which I'm being considered, and observative.)
2. It offend others (which I'm being considered, and observative.)
3. That's dangerous and hurt the next individual.
4. Dis-respectful

Let's see what the Lord say about people whom offend others.

Matthew 18:16-But whoever causes one of these little ones who believe in Me to sin, it would be better for him if a millstone were hung around his neck, and he were drowned in the depth of the sea.

What does Lord say about teasing others is he please with that? That we'll see.

Ephesians 5:4-Neither filthiness, nor foolish talking, nor jesting, which are not convenient: but rather giving of thanks. The question about is the Lord really please with that? The answer is No.

Romans 15:1-We then that are strong ought to bear the infirmities of the weak, and not to please ourselves.

Verse:2-Let every one of us please his neighbor for his good to edification.

I Corinthians 8:12-But when ye sin so against the brethren and wound their weak conscience, ye sin against Christ. Verse:13-Wherefore, if meat make my brother to offend, I will eat no flesh while the world standeth, lest I make my brother to offend.

1. Be considered of others.
2. Respect the feelings of others.
3. Respect the wish of other.
4. Treat others the way you wish to be treated.
5. Be understandable.

Matthew 5:9-Blessed are the peacemakers: for they shall be called the children of God.

Life full of ups and downs

How often shall I forgive others?

Matthew 18:21-Then came Peter to him, and said, Lord, how oft shall my brother sin against me, and I forgive him? Till seven times?

Verse:22-Jesus saith unto him, I say no unto thee until seven times: But, until seventy times seven.

Should we take revenge?

What does scriptures say about taking revenge? Should we or should we not take revenge on people did us wrong? The answer the fleshly side of us seeking revenge, don't want to forgive others.

Romans 12:17-Recompense to no man evil for evil, Provide things honest in the sight of all men.

Verse:19-Dearly beloved, avenge not yourselves, but rather give place unto wrath: for it is written, vengence is mine; I will repay, saith the Lord.

Verse:20-Therefore if thine enemy hunger, feed him; if he thirst, give him drink; for in so doing thou shalt heap coals of fire on his head.

Verse:21-Be not overcome of evil, but overcome evil with good.

Life full of ups and downs

Life full of ups and downs
where did it came from?
How did it happen?

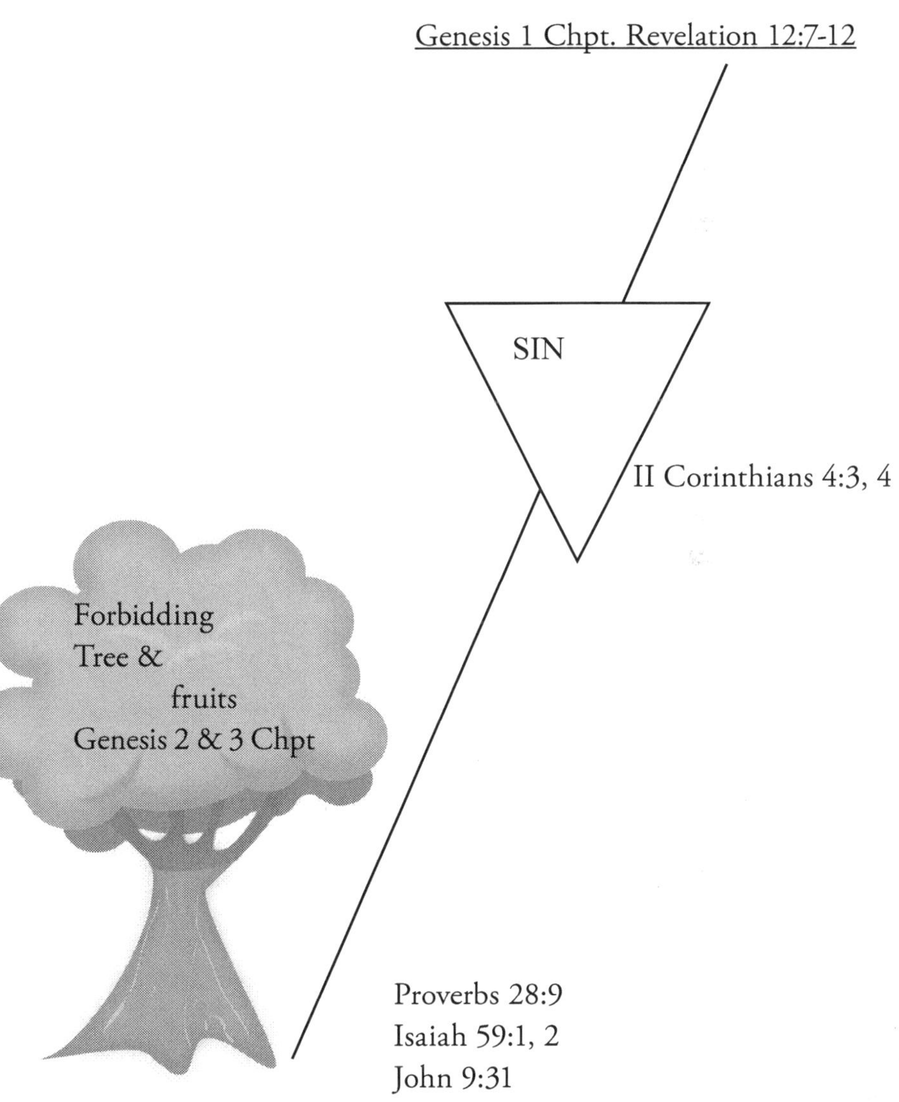

Life full of ups and downs

Back in the Relationship with God

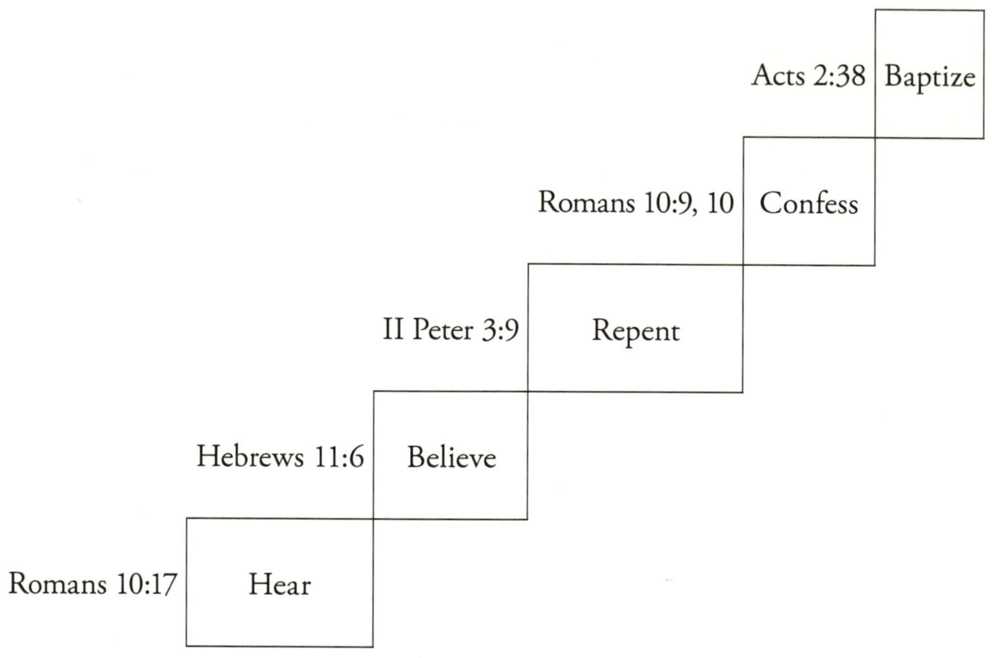

What is sin? I John 3:4-Whosoever committeth sin transgresseth also the law: for sin is the transgression of the law.

Verse:5-And ye know that he was manifested to take away our sins; and in him is no sin.

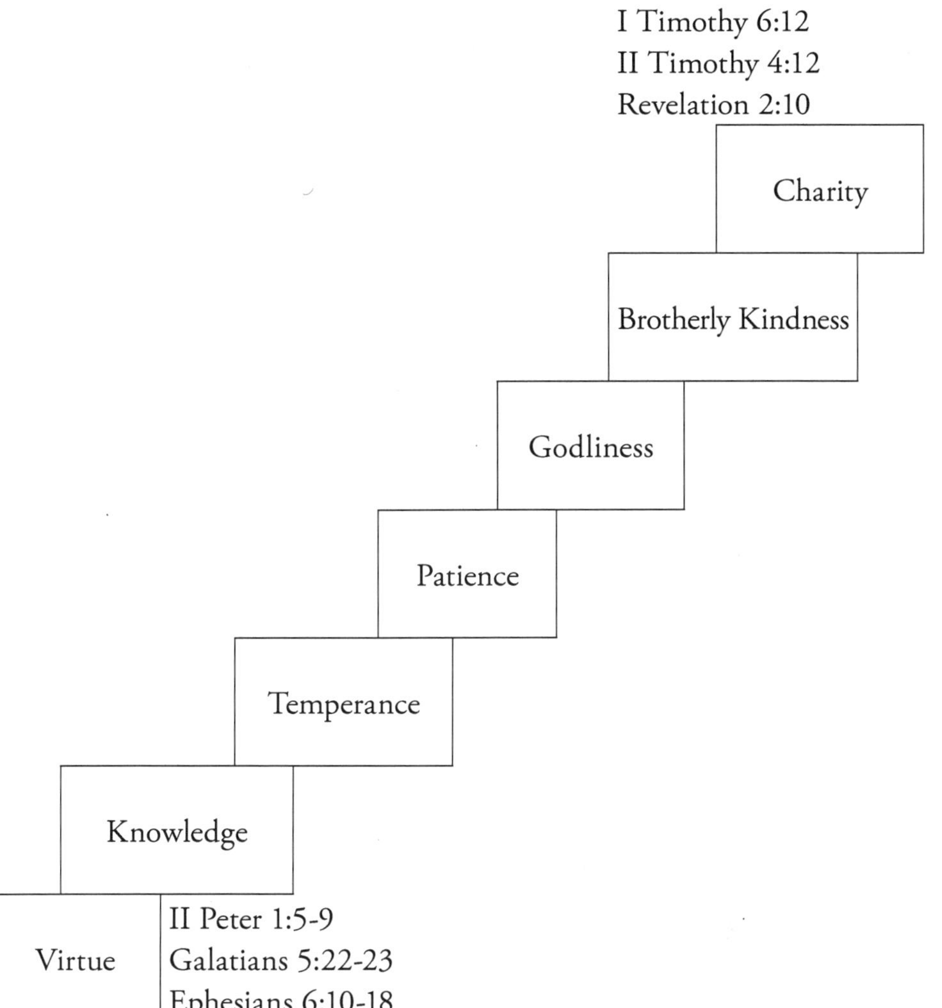
I Timothy 6:12
II Timothy 4:12
Revelation 2:10
Charity
Brotherly Kindness
Godliness
Patience
Temperance
Knowledge
Virtue
II Peter 1:5-9
Galatians 5:22-23
Ephesians 6:10-18

Life full of ups and downs

You are now running the race

Hebrews 12:2

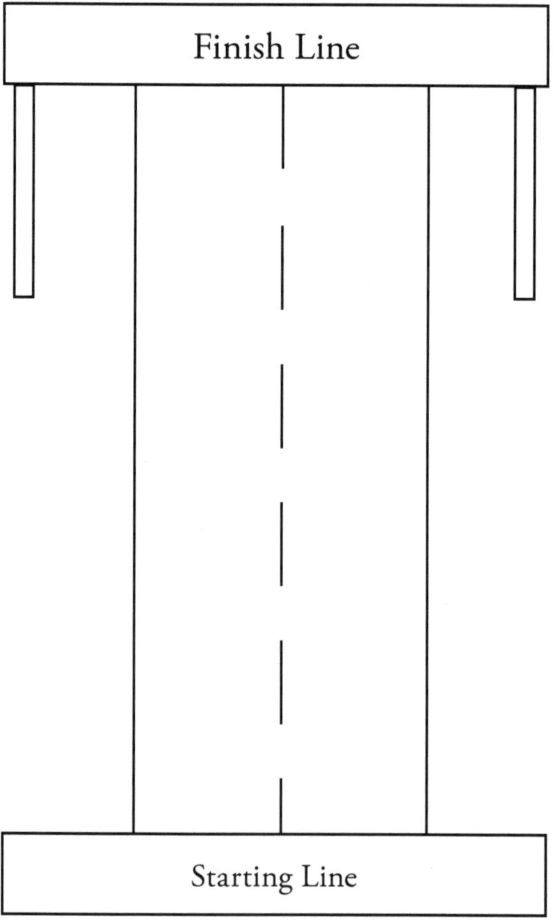

Matthew 16:24 Romans 12:2 I Corinthians 9:24-27
Philippians 3:13, 14

Life full of ups and downs

Build your hopes on things eternal Hebrews 11:1

I Corinthians 3:9-11
Ephesian 2:19-22
I Peter 2:5
I Timothy 3:16
Colossians 1:23
Colossians 2:6, 7

Life full of ups and downs

In the time of discouragement

In the world of discouragement
What are we discouragement on?

1. Something that meet our interest
2. Something that meet our happiness
3. Something that meet our likeness
4. Something that meet our satisfactory
5. Something that meet our plans

All 5 of these that were name seem to be taken from us
You hath to put forth effort to earn these yourself; for as earn it yourself you more better off because it's your.

I remember what David said in Psalm 27:14 (wait on the Lord: be of good courage, and he shall strengthen thine heart: wait, I say, on the Lord.)

To us in the time of discouragement God may not come when we want him but, he's right on time.

Life full of ups and downs

Do God give us everything we want?

Do God give us everything we want? Notice what David said in Psalms 23:1-(The Lord is my shepherd; I shall not want.)

When we want something, and don't come our way as we wish we quickly get inpatient do something we regret.

James 1:3-Knowing that the testing of your faith produces patience.

Verse:4-But let patience have its perfect work, that you may be perfect and complete, lacking nothing.

Keep Asking, Seeking, Knocking

Matthew 7:7-"Ask, and it will be given to you: seek, and you will find: knock, and it will be opened to you.

Verse:8-"For everyone who asks receives, and he who seeks finds, and to him who knocks it will be opened.

Verse:9-"Or what man is there among you who, if his son asks for bread, will give him a stone?

Verse:10-"Or if he ask for a fish, will he give him a serpent?

Will God supply our needs?

Philippians 4:19-And my God shall supply all your need according to his riches in glory by Christ Jesus.

The question will God supply all our need? The answer is yes

Life full of ups and downs

In time of depression

Things involve depression

1.) Feeling Hopeless

2.) Feel that you in the world by yourself

3.) Lack of happiness

4.) Lack of interest

5.) Lack of satisfaction

6.) Lack of communication

7.) Being treated less

8.) Your desire being taken from you

9.) Feel like you loosing something

10.) You are being neglected by others

11.) Being look down on

12.) One think one better than other

13.) Envying one another

14.) Dis-liking one another

15.) Drinking themselves away

16.) <u>Gambling</u>

17.) <u>Drug Related</u>

18.) <u>Suicide</u>

19.) <u>Not seeing eye to eye with each other</u>

20.) <u>Back biting</u>

21.) <u>Pity Party the blues</u>

22.) <u>Expect everybody stoop down your level</u>

23.) <u>Worrying about things you got no control over</u>

24.) <u>Worries too much</u>

25.) <u>Self-fish</u>

26.) <u>Boastful</u>

Life full of ups and downs

"Facing the real world"

Facing the real world; yes we're obligated to face the real world this life is feel with sorrow, and trouble here below we often made to wonder just why it should be so, and every tribulation this life must bring to view O Lord we need a friend like you. There are life full of disappointment, full of discouragement, full of depression, full of trial and tribulation, full of trouble; things don't go our way like we want to, and we sometime don't know to be patient; remember the familiar hymn (Take your burden to the Lord and leave it there.) There's another hymn that brighten our day: (Trust and obey for there's no other way to be in Jesus but to trust, and obey.) The correct saying in the hymn in song <u>Trust and Obey</u> (to be happy in Jesus but to trust and obey.) We got a everlasting arm to lean on the familiar hymn (what a fellowship what a joy divine leaning on the everlasting arm.)

Each day we got to lean on him trouble don't last always. We know how we came in this world but we don't know how we leaving we don't have no choice I remember when I was growing up I heard a song (you got to move when the Lord call your name you got to move) we all got to give account for our self to the Lord. Romans 14:12

John 3:16-"For God so loved the world that he gave his only begotten Son, that whosoever believes in Him shall not perish but have everlasting life.

Yes salvation has been brought down it took place on Mount Calvary cruel Calvary.

I once was lost in sin but Jesus took me in and then a little light from heaven filled my soul; It bathed my heart in love and wrote my name above, now just a little talk through Jesus makes me whole. I may have doubts and fears, my eyes be filled with tears, but Jesus is a friend who watches day and night; I go to God in prayer he knows my every care, and just a little talk through Jesus makes it right. Have a little talk through Jesus tell God all about our trouble hear our faintest cry answer by and by feel a little prayerful yearning heart unto heaven is turning find a little talk through Jesus makes it right.

You are now in the real world, you are facing the real world, the world of right and wrong, you got a decision to make out of 1 of the 2 the road can be highways or die ways the choice is your. 1968 Copyright David Ruffin and the Temptations wrote the song (Cloud Nine) that one of my favorites (You can be what you want to be you got your own responsibility.)

Life full of ups and downs

Shelter in the time of storm

You may feel hopeless you may feel forsaken

Hebrews 13:5-Let your conversation be without covetousness: be content with such things as you have. For He Himself has said, “I will never leave thee nor forsake thee.”

Life full of ups and downs

What are your hope build on?

Remind me in the familiar hymn (My hope is build on nothing lest but Jesus blood and righteousness.)

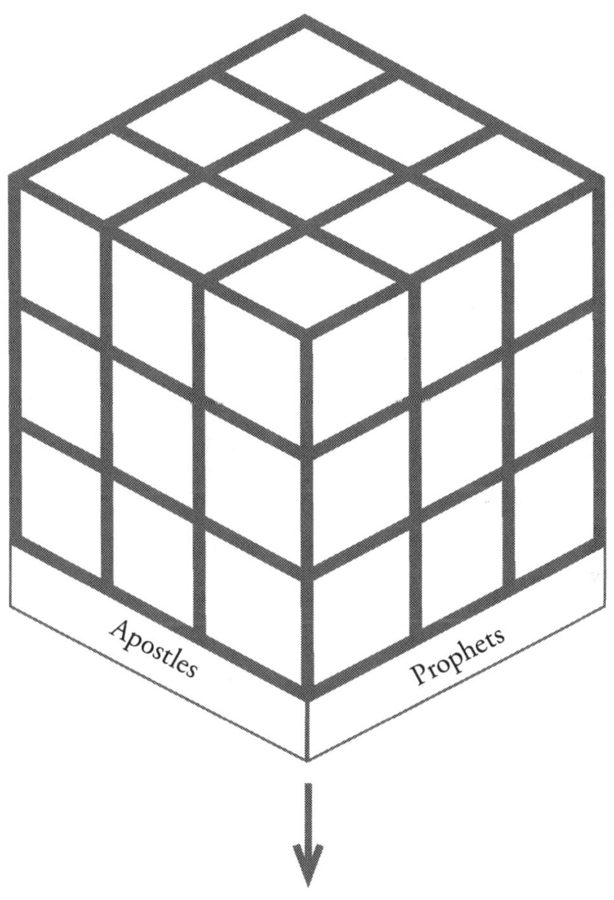

Jesus Christ
Cornerstone
Ephesians 2:20

Life full of ups and downs

Tongue and Teeth fallout sometime

Have you ever heard the saying tongue and teeth fall out some time? I heard a saying like this (It be that way some time.)

I remember eating a cube steak and accidently bit my tongue that what you call tongue and teeth fall out. Even friends fall out with each other, family members fall out with each other; church family members fall out with each other.

I remember growing up me, and my cousins were play-mate what a good we really love one another we were taught that; I remember one day we got into a fight daddy came home from work how he solve the problem he gave everyone of us a quarter for ice cream sandwich after that we forgotten what we fighting for; we got along just like that.

Look at the church in Corinth there were great division among themselves Paul's letter to them.

I Corinthians 1:10-Now I beseech you, brethren, by the name of our Lord Jesus Christ, that ye all speak the same thing, and that there be no divisions among you; but that ye be perfectly joined together in the same mind and in the same judgment.

When I was growing up I got in plenty of fights with my siblings it all because we didn't see eye to eye with each other it seem more like cats and dogs fight I don't know which one of us the cat, and which one of us the dog; but I will say this we might fight like cats and dogs but don't lay a hand on us.

The question do cats and dogs always fight? The answer no it's a some time thing. I remember I was 8 years old going on 9 years old I once had a dog name Rusty one Saturday night me and my dad took Rusty out for a walk to my aunt's house my cousin live across the street from my aunt he had this dog name Tiger, he came out of nowhere and jumped on Rusty I got mad with him I kicked him hard and told him get off my dog howling, back in his yard. I came home from one I saw laying on my front porch and thought that was Rusty, I said to myself I know what he doing here; they turn out to be friends. That's point about tongue and teeth fall out sometime; sometime married have dis-agreement, even someone you dating have dis-agreement, them who dating don't drop each other like hot potatoe because you have dis-agreement straight it out with love.

Everyday not peaches and cream, some days sour pickle and cream that's not a good combination.

Life full of ups and downs

Joy cometh in the morning

Psalm 30:5-For his anger is but for a moment, His favor is for life; weeping may endure for a night, but joy comes in the morning.

Here's another familiar hymn it pick you up why you down; (on Christ the solid rock I stand.)

I thought about that hymn it's a uplift to me; I got another favorite (Happy Summer land of bliss)

Whatever you going through trouble don't last always.

Romans 8:31-What the shall we say to these things? If God is for us, who can be against us?

Verse:35-Who shall separate us from the love of Christ? Shall tribulation, or distress, or peril, or sword?

Psalm 19:14-Let the words of my mouth and the meditation of my heart, Be acceptable in thy sight O Lord, my strength and my Redeemer.

Life full of ups and downs

"Take no thought for tomorrow"

Take no thought for tomorrow June 19th, 1982 the night never forgotten I was taught the truth by family members my aunt, uncle, host of my cousins this when it took place the evening I was taught the truth the same evening I was baptize, that was a shocking news to them it sound a bomb from Williston to Allendale, S.C. I urge anyone take no thought for tomorrow it's not promise. I remember growing up heard a song (May be the last time I don't know)

Matthew 6:34-Take therefore no thought for the morrow: for the morrow shall take thought for the things of itself. Sufficient unto the day is the evil thereof.

James 4:14 Where as ye know not what shall be on the morrow. For what is your life? It is even a vapour, that appeareth for a little time, and then vanisheth away.

Verse:15-For that ye ought to say, If the Lord's will, we shall live, and do this, or that.

On my job when time to clock-out I tell my boss I'll see you tomorrow if the Lord's will.
My boss man he ask me why I do say that? I told him I may go to sleep and might not wake-up to see the next day, the next day not promise.

Life full of ups and downs

"Lean on me"

1972 Bill Withers wrote the song Lean on me this song inspires me a great deal; I been through time of tragedy lost two siblings in March 1972 the same week I was 10 years old going on 11 years old when it happen my second oldest brother was in Air force station in Thailand he was kill off duty, at the same week my sister was missing from her home later during that week she was found dead in back of her house.

That song (Lean on me) help me a great deal encourage me to get on in life; I remember the familiar hymn it was my sister's (God be with you til we meet again) we will but not on this side but on the other side that's a promise

Life full of ups and downs

"Win by losing"

In this life there's winning by losing, as losing we learn from it; the mistake we make we learn also from it. You win some, and lose some.

Ecclesiastes 3:1-To everything there is a reason, and a time to every purpose under the heaven:

Verse:6-A time to get and a time to lose; a time to keep, and a time to cast away;

In Christ Jesus are the victory won?

I Corinthians 15:57-But thanks be to God, who gives us the victory through our Lord Jesus Christ.

The question are the victory won? The answer is yes the victory won.

Hebrews 10:17 "Their sins and iniquity will I remember no more."

Verse:18-Now where there is remission of these, these is no longer an offering for sin.

Isaiah spoke in time pass concerning savior, and the victory:

Isaiah 53:5-But He was wounded for our transgressions, He was bruised for our iniquities; The chastisement for our peace was upon Him, And by His stripes we are healed.

"You are free indeed by the blood"

Life full of ups and downs

"Evil communication corrupts good manners"

The time I was growing up I wasn't around a lots of guys my age most of the time I been around old folks sit there, and hear them talk; I heard some things interet me a great deal; that's how I learn family history my ancestor even way back in the doors of time; I learned the rest of it of my own I trace way back to Gambia, West Africa which is now call in time James Island it's a new name call today Kunta Kinta Island; it was name after him because he was a strongest warrior someone who stood tall in his culture; those I learn on my own; some family member gave me a nick name the nick-name (Walking History Book) if it don't be that its (Walking Archives.) My first cousin brought me a book on family history she must have known all that time that I'm gone be a writer and it finally came true it was host of my cousin on both sides of my family knew that; their a lot of admires from both sides they stood by me thick, and thin; getting back to evil communication parents and guardians they hoped and prayed the I wouldn't get involve with drugs and alcohol their prayers were answer.

Their prayer were answered I didn't never smoke nor drink, they prayed that I don't get involve with the wrong crowd; guest what I didn't; where I was raise in Cayce, S.C. lots of people know I stayed to myself a lot didn't bother anybody easy to get along with but one thing not to take for granted, and my easy going for weakness.

I Corinthians 15:33-Be not deceived: evil communication corrupts good manners.

II Corinthians 6:17-Wherefore come out from among them, and be ye separate, saith the Lord, and touch not the unclean thing; and I will receive you,

Verse:18-And will be a Father unto you, And ye shall be my sons and daughters, saith the Almighty.

I remember when I was in high school never been in trouble, never got written up I was accuse of something I didn't do, and some one who know me well stood up, and said Cedric didn't do anything wrong.

I remember in my sophomore year in high school I came in contact with a bully I tried to avoid him; he was bully me around; I tried to walk away from him, he knock the books out of my hand, he said some sexual thing about my mother I was boiling mad I jack him up to the pole I was about to give a hard left-hand my neighbor, and restrain from him he took it over, and gave him a good licking.

Life full of ups and downs

Everybody not gonna like the same thing PT-1

Everybody different from each other; I may like cowboy boots you might not like cowboy boots; I may like bib-overall you might not; I may 4 door cars, and trucks, you may 2 door car, and trucks; does that mean we can't get along, and except each as we are? Everybody not gonna like the same thing.

The question do everybody like North, East, South, West? The answer there's some Do's and Don'ts.

The question about automobiles do everybody like Chevrolet? Do everybody like Ford, Do everybody like Dodge? The answer no everybody not gonna like the same thing; Everybody don't have the same taste. Every farmer don't plant a garden alike it don't mean whose right, whose wrong; every farmer not alike but they still know what they doing

I learned how to farm when I was 7 years old going on 8 years my dad taught me so did 2 of my uncles on my mother's side of the family, and I'm still farming today but thank God I'm a country boy, and a southerner.

Things I told my mom, and dad I guest they never hear that from me, I been trying to tell them that for the longest, and it went through; I told them I'm glad that I wasn't raise up North if that would've been the case I could've been a jailbird with a short life I told them they chose to stay in the South which that was a wise choice.

They were surprise when they heard me said that; my dad ask me and said do you really mean that? I told him yes I do you know I don't smoke, and drank he was proud when I said that.

I remember when Uncle Chester, and Uncle Henry came up this way I was in the kitchen helping mother prepare meal, and they done pull up in the yard already they came in we greeted one another we were getting ready for dinner holding good conversation; Uncle Henry ask me how my work going I said great; and mother told him and said Dale really tried hard he put alots of effort in what he do, and my dad yes he really tries hard; when he studies he studies, even stays up late at night I've never seen him like that. About what my parents were telling they were right.

P.S. I hope you enjoyed what you read I hope you encouragement out this and help as it help me have a blessed day. Remember the saying (Live and Let Live)

Made in the USA
Columbia, SC
27 October 2024